The Pocket Book of
Baby Massage

Anita Epple & Pauline Carpenter

Published and distributed in Great Britain by Ditto International Ltd, 7 Regent's Hall, St Mary's Avenue, Stony Stratford, Buckinghamshire, MK11 1EB.

Acknowledgments

Many thanks to Nicci Blackman and baby Foster.

Contents

Introduction

Welcome to this pocket-sized baby massage book! It has been specially designed for busy parents who want to learn how to massage their baby using an easy, no-nonsense, step-by-step guide.

Whether you're looking to help your baby overcome colic, disturbed sleep or just want to enhance your special time

together, the benefits of baby massage are enormous and can involve the whole family. Massage can also help you to learn how your baby is communicating with you, creating a sense of security and feelings of love and respect.

This little book is filled with simple instructions for a full body massage for your baby, tips, hints and nursery rhymes and yet is small enough to slip into your pocket. The massage is simple to follow and will take only 20 minutes to complete once you're familiar with all the strokes. If you can, we recommend a full massage each day, however, the beauty of massage is that, not only can it be as short or as long as your baby wants, but it can also be done almost anywhere.

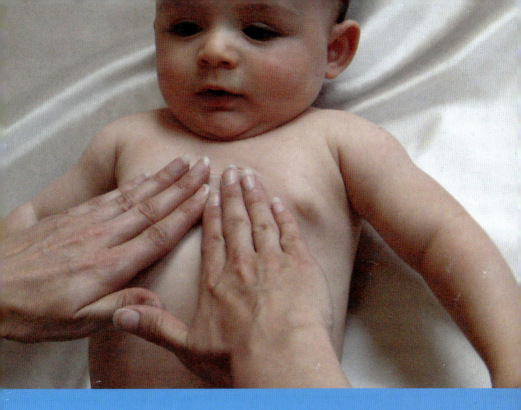

We feel privileged to share with you this passion of ours and a skill that we hope will change your lives, just as it has changed ours. Our sincerest congratulations on deciding to practise one of the simplest, yet most important activities that can not only help your baby to grow emotionally and physically, but is also great fun!

Anita & Pauline

The benefits ✓

Benefits of receiving massage

Massage can help a baby:

- Adapt to their new environment and become generally more settled

- Learn to interact and play with others

- Feel loved, respected and secure

Massage can also:

- Stimulate all the senses

- Promote relaxation which can improve quality of sleep

- Regulate the digestive system and reduce the discomfort of colic, wind and constipation

- Strengthen the respiratory and immune systems

- Stimulate the circulatory system and help balance the nervous system

- Enhance growth and development

- Encourage body awareness

- Improve skin condition and muscle tone

- Maintain flexibility of the joints, ligaments and tendons

Benefits of giving massage

Massage can help parents:

- Become more confident and competent in handling their baby

- Understand what their baby is 'saying to them' *(non-verbal cues)*

- Relax whilst having fun with their baby

- Develop a feeling of closeness with their baby

- Find time to play constructively with their baby, so that the relationship may strengthen and grow

Massage can also:

- Encourage lactation through the stimulation of Prolactin

- Encourage the nurturing instinct through the stimulation of Oxytocin

- Help with sibling rivalry *(gets older children involved)*

- Be adapted so all family members can benefit!

Finding the best time to massage your baby

Age of baby

From birth prepare your baby for massage with lots of loving cuddles; giving them time to adjust to their new environment. As they develop, slowly introduce long, sweeping strokes over your baby's clothes which will gently accustom them to massage. When your baby is about six weeks old they should be ready to start experiencing a longer, more structured massage routine.

Once crawling your baby might not be interested in regular massage, but don't despair they should become interested again at about 18 months old.

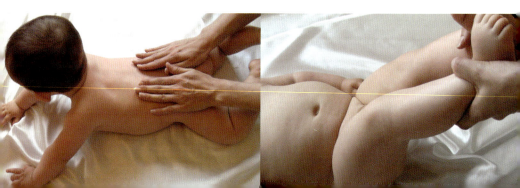

Best time for baby and you

To really enjoy the massage your baby should be alert and happy. Listen to and observe how your baby is responding to the massage. If they seem unhappy at all consider trying a different stroke. If this doesn't work then try massaging at another time when they are more content and are saying 'yes' to a massage.

Choose a time that is also right for you!

When you might have to avoid massaging your baby

When a baby:

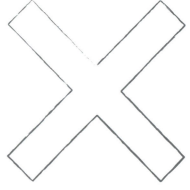

- Has just been fed. *(The digestive system needs at least 45 minutes to digest food before massage can begin)*

- Is asleep, tired, hungry, crying or fretful. *(These are all 'no' cues)*

- Is unwell, or has a raised temperature. *(Massage would be too stimulating for the immune system)*

- Has had vaccinations within the previous three days. *(Vaccinations have an impact on the immune system, so massage would be far too stimulating during this time)*

Also if a baby has:

- Undergone recent surgery. *(Avoid massaging the affected area for at least eight weeks)*

- An infectious skin condition. *(Massage may aggravate the infected area, or spread the condition)*

- Any bruises, weeping wounds, rashes, or a sore navel. *(Refrain from massage until the affected area has completely healed)*

- Jaundice. *(Refrain from massage until the liver is functioning properly)*

- Suffered haemorrhaging. *(As massage increases the blood flow in the body and there may be a risk of further bleeding)*

- Been diagnosed with brittle bone disease. *(The bones may be so brittle that they break with normal handling)*

If you have any medical concerns about your baby please seek advice from a doctor of physician before using massage.

Massage oils

Oils to use

The best oils for massage are cold-pressed vegetable oils such as:

✓ **Sunflower:** the oil that is closest to the oil in the human skin

✓ **Grapeseed:** a stable oil and less likely to go off

✓ **Olive:** has antiseptic properties but is viscous and likely to mark clothing. Fine when diluted with sunflower oil

✓ **Fractionated coconut:** good for a baby with a suppressed immune system *(Maybe difficult to find.)*

Pour about a teaspoon full of oil in the palm of your hand and rub hands together to warm the oil prior to massage. Reapply oil as needed to prevent friction, but not so much that your baby is too slippery.

Store oil in a cool, dark place and throw it away if you suspect it has gone rancid.

Oils to avoid!

X **Mineral:** stops the skin from breathing and can dry the skin out when used regularly

X **Nut and wheat germ:** can provoke an allergic reaction

X **Mustard:** is quite toxic

X **Essential:** these are too potent to use on a regular basis for baby massage

Singing with massage

It is really important to talk and sing to your baby and this is particularly suited to massage time.

Benefits:

- Enhances the communication between you and your baby

- Babies respond positively to rhythm and repetition such as found in nursery rhymes

- Singing rhymes with your baby can be soothing and comforting

- Helps with baby's speech and language development

- Boosts brain development

Each stroke in this book is accompanied with a nursery rhyme, giving you the opportunity to talk and sing with your baby as you massage them.

In time your child will be humming and eventually singing along with you!

Getting prepared

Before any massage begins it is important to make sure that the environment is just right to create a peaceful atmosphere.

The room

When preparing the massage space the room should be:

Warm: So your baby is comfortable when undressed for the massage.

Light: Ideally natural daylight or soft lamps to avoid the need for bright over-head lighting.

Quiet: To create a relaxing ambiance for you and your baby with minimal distractions. Free from strong smells and preferably with soothing music.

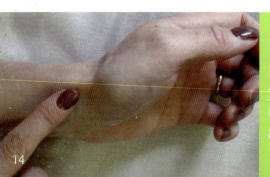

Patch test the oil

Rub a small amount of oil on you and your baby's wrist and leave for 15 minutes. If there is a reaction, wash off gently and test a different vegetable oil.

The equipment

Before the massage begins gather the essential items:

This Book!!

CD player and relaxing music.

Change mat and towels.

Massage oil.

Tissues and baby wipes.

A drink for baby when massage is over.

And you

Not only do you need to prepare the room, the equipment and your baby, but you need to be prepared too!

Wear comfortable clothing.

Remove jewellery that may scratch.

Wash hands and check nails for snags.

Tie long hair back.

Think about your comfort when sitting on the floor.

The massage

Recommended sequence for practising massage:

- The legs

- The tummy

- The chest, arms and hands

- The head and face

- The back

We recommend that you introduce massage gradually to your baby. Starting with the legs allows your baby to become accustomed to the strokes as they are the least sensitive part of their body. Each week, introduce a new section and practise the previous week's strokes until you build up to a full massage in about 5 weeks.

Before you begin massaging your baby it is vital that you 'ask permission' from your baby to see if they would like a massage. This is a sign that your baby will soon come to recognise and it gives them the opportunity to say 'no' if it is not the right time to massage. We know this seems odd at first! Bear with it – it soon becomes quite natural.

Asking permission

- Whilst your baby is still clothed place your hands lightly on their chest

- Rub gently in a circular motion and ask your baby 'Would you like a massage *(name)*?'

- If your baby is saying 'yes', start with the Velvet Cloak

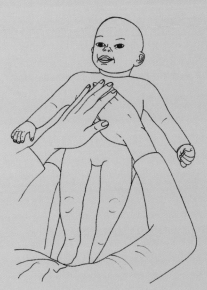

Velvet cloak

To begin and end all massage sessions

- Bring both hands to the top of your baby's head

- Use the flat of your whole hand, lightly stroke down the sides of their body to the feet

- Repeat 3 times

- Undress your baby.

Now for the massage.................

Upward leg glide

Stroke firmly towards the heart and gently away from the heart

Jack and Jill
Went up the hill
To fetch a pail of water

Jack fell down
And broke his crown
And Jill came tumbling after!

BENEFIT: This is good for relaxing the muscles

- Support your baby's leg by cupping the ankle with one hand

- Glide your other hand up the side of the leg from the ankle to the top of the thigh

- Cup around the back of the thigh and return your hand to the ankle

- Swap hands and glide up the other side of the leg

- Repeat 3 times with both hands

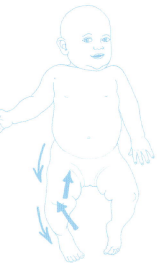

Gentle leg knead

 Do not put any pressure on the knee and stroke gently away from the heart

 One potato,
Two potato,
Three potato,
Four.
Five potato
Six potato,
Seven potato more!

BENEFIT: Good for circulation

- Still support your baby's leg with one hand

- With the other hand cup the fingers at the back of the leg

- Using the pad of the thumb knead the top of the leg on one side up towards the knee

- Gently glide the thumb over the knee

- Continue to knead from just above the knee to the hip

- Glide your hand back to the ankle

- Swap hands and knead up the other side of the leg

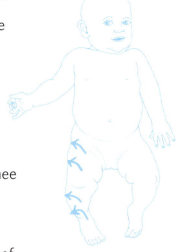

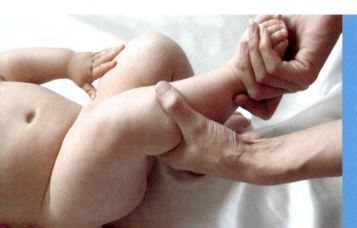

Repeat the The Upward Leg Glide and Gentle Leg Knead on the other leg before moving on to the feet

Sole stroke

 Take care not to tickle and only use the pads of the thumbs, not the tips

Windscreen wipers
What do you do all day?
Swish, swosh
Swish, swosh
I wipe the rain away

Windscreen wipers
What do you do all day?
Swish, swosh
Swish, swosh
I wipe the rain away

BENEFIT: Opens up the energy channels in the reflexology zones

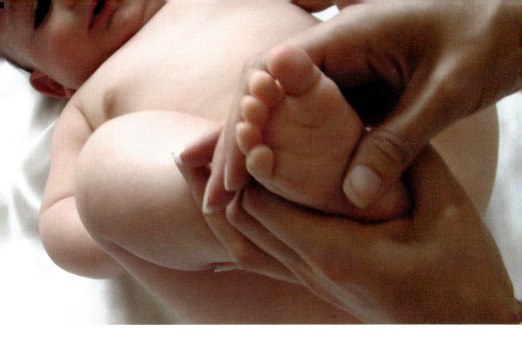

- Still supporting the slightly raised leg

- Stroke the sole of the foot, from heel to toes, alternating the thumbs from one side to the other

- Repeat 3 times

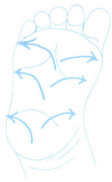

Bubbling springs

Watch your baby to check that they are happy with the pressure.
Only use the pad of the thumb

BENEFIT: Reduces stress and helps baby to feel relaxed

Round and round the garden
Like a teddy bear
One step, two step
And kiss you under there
(kiss under the toes)

- Cup the front of the foot with one hand

- With the other hand gently press your thumb into the soft spot in the centre of the foot *(just below the pads)*

- Do this for the length of the rhyme and release

- Can be repeated 3 times

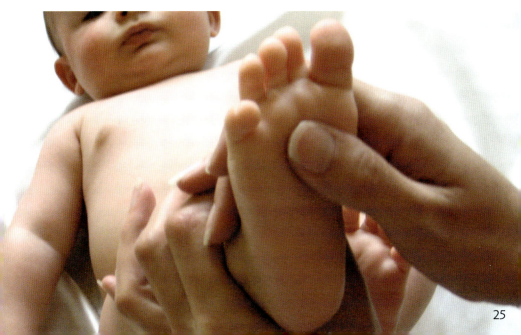

Toe rolling

 Do not twist the toes. The pull at the end of each toe should be gentle

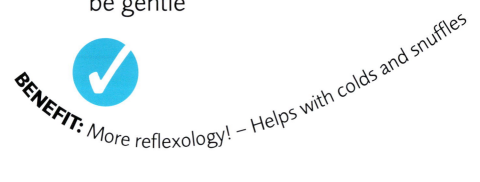

BENEFIT: *More reflexology! – Helps with colds and snuffles*

Starting with the big toe:
This little piggy went to market
This little piggy stayed at home
This little piggy had a massage
And this little piggy didn't want one
And this little piggy said
'Oh, oh, oh I want one too!'

- Still supporting the slightly raised leg

- Starting with the big toe, gently roll your finger and thumb from the base of the toe to the tip *(so the action resembles a caterpillar)*

- Gently pull each toe at the end of the roll

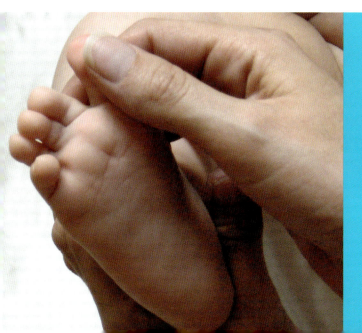

Now repeat all the foot strokes on the other foot

Ankle soother

 Use the pads of the thumbs only. Hold the foot securely during the stroke

 Hot cross buns
Hot cross buns
One a penny
Two a penny
Hot cross buns

BENEFIT: Improves circulation to the joints

- Cup the heel with both hands

- Stroke the top of the ankle, using the thumbs, from the middle to the sides

- Repeat 3 times

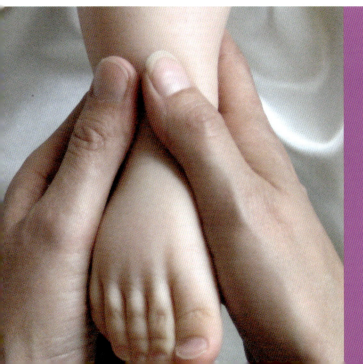

Repeat The Upward Leg Glide (page 18) on this leg

Now repeat The Ankle Soother and Upward Leg Glide on the other leg

Jelly roll

 It is important not to roll the knee and the ankle joints. If you have large hands only use the first two fingers. Babies really love this stroke, so sing the rhyme with gusto!

Jelly on a plate
Jelly on a plate
Wibble wobble,
wibble wobble
Jelly on a plate

Jelly on a plate
Jelly on a plate
Wibble wobble,
wibble wobble
Jelly on a plate

BENEFIT: Relaxes the leg by literally 'rolling out' tension

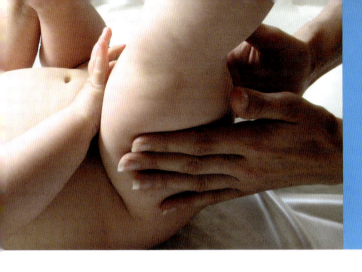

- Support one of your baby's legs upright by holding the thigh between both hands *(as though making a dough sausage)*

- Roll the thigh between both hands *to verse1*

- Gently slide hands over the knee to the calf

- Roll the calf *to verse 2*

- Repeat once more

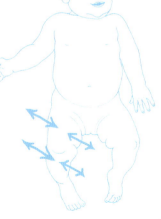

31

Double leg lift

 Do not lift your baby's bottom off the mat.
Take care to stroke gently down the back of the legs

BENEFIT: A lovely way to end the leg massage

 Leg over leg,
As the dog went to Dover;
When he came to a stile
Hop! He went over.

- From the sides, slide your hands under your baby's bottom

- Gently stroke down the back of the legs to the ankles, lifting the legs gently as you go

- Gently lower the legs

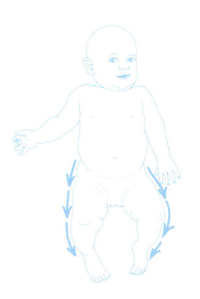

Tummy hug

 Remember to try and keep one of your hands constantly on your baby

Pizza, Pizza – it's a treat.
Pizza, pizza – fun to eat!
Stringy, gooey cheese so yummy;
Pepperoni in my tummy.
Pizza, pizza – it's a treat.
Pizza, pizza – fun to eat!

BENEFIT: This is a lovely warming stroke to begin the tummy massage

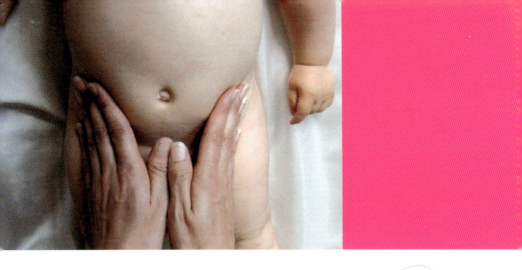

- Mould your hands around your baby's lower back and sides (take care not to lift their back from the floor)

- Glide both hands to the front of the tummy just below the navel

- Repeat 3 times

Tummy circle

 Massage the tummy in a clockwise direction only. Do not work on the ribcage.

BENEFIT: A good stroke to start to get things moving in the tummy!

Babies tummies are nice and round
Make a lovely gurgling sound
A massage by my super mummy
(or daddy or granny)
Helps me have a happy tummy!

- Using the pads of 2 fingers draw a wide circle around your baby's tummy button

- Repeat 3 times

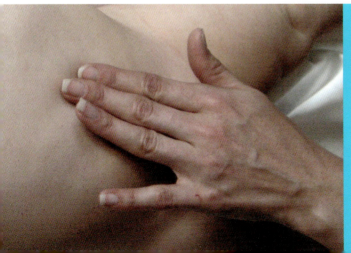

Daisy wheel

 Still working clockwise make sure the strokes are below the ribcage

Roses are red
They smell yummy
Daisies are white
All over my tummy

BENEFIT: *A good stroke to help move trapped wind*

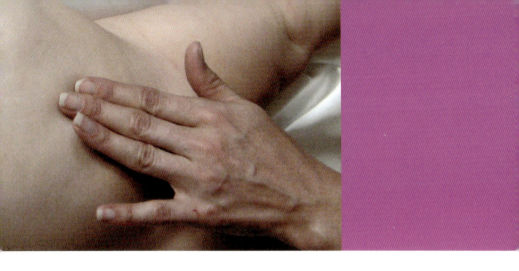

- Using the pads of 2 fingers make small circles like the petals of a flower around your baby's tummy, following the line of the tummy circle

- Repeat 3 times

- Finish with a complete Tummy Circle

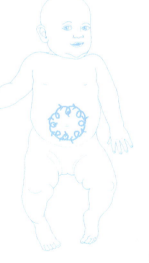

Tummy square

 Still working clockwise, lighten the pressure over the bladder

BENEFIT: *A good stroke to alleviate constipation*

 Doctor Foster went to Gloucester
In a shower of rain.
He stepped in a puddle
Right up to his middle,
And never went there again

- Following the line of the Tummy Circle, add corners and draw a square on your baby's tummy

- Repeat 3 times

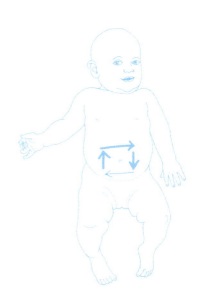

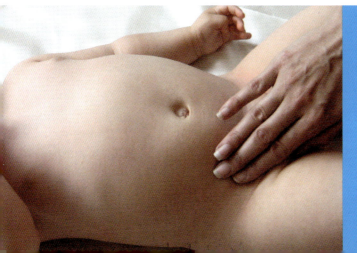

Windmill

 Lighten the pressure over the bladder

BENEFIT: A good stroke to alleviate colic

Blow wind blow
And go mill go
That the Miller may grind his corn

That the Baker may take it
And into bread make it
And bring us a loaf in the morn

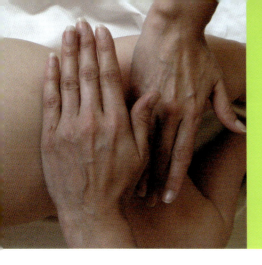

- Imagine your hands are like two paddles

- Stroke down one hand at a time from below your baby's rib cage to the top of the legs *(like the sails on a windmill)*

- Repeat 3 times with each hand

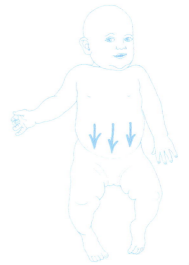

Knee hug

 Don't force your baby's legs if they resist

 Easy peasy
Nice and easy
Stretch your legs
And bend your kneesy!

BENEFIT: *A classic yoga move which may release trapped wind!*

- Hold both legs just above your baby's ankles

- Gently bend their legs at the knee and bring the thighs up towards their tummy

- Hold for a count of 6

- Relax the legs down again

- Repeat 3 times

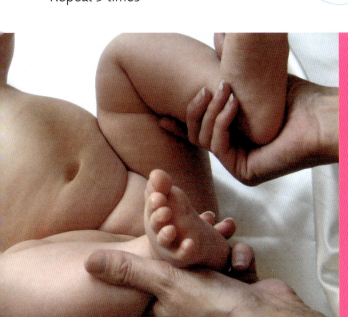

Chest and arm glide

 Take care not to start below the ribs

BENEFIT: A good stroke to put oil on the chest and arms

Mary had a little lamb
Its fleece was white as snow
And everywhere that Mary went
The lamb was sure to go

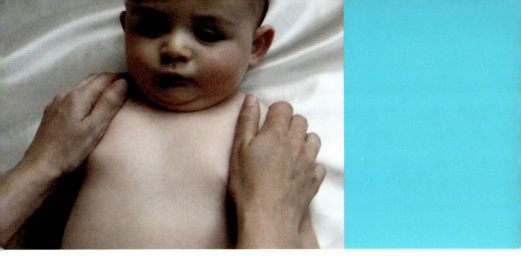

- Place both of your hands flat on your baby's chest

- Slide your hands up the chest

- Cup the shoulders

- Gently stroke down their arms to the wrists

- Finish by opening their palms gently with your thumbs *(if they let you!)*

- Repeat 3 times

Loving heart

 Only work on the chest

 BENEFIT: A relaxing and toning stroke

 Hickory Dickory Dock,
The mouse ran up the clock;
The clock struck one
And down he did run,
Hickory Dickory Dock

- Using both hands, form a heart shape on your baby's chest by:

- Gliding the pads of the fingers up the middle of the chest towards the neck

- Part your hands and gently sweep back down again

- Repeat 3 times

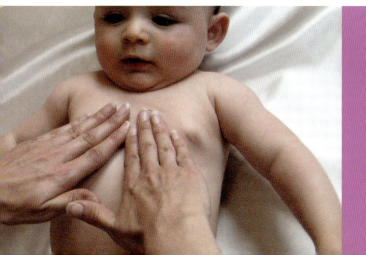

Loving kisses

 Avoid tickling your baby when massaging under the arms

 BENEFIT: Good for general health and well-being

Hot cross buns
Hot cross buns
One a penny
Two a penny
Hot cross buns

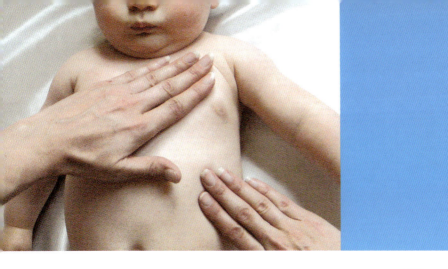

- Place both of your hands either side of your baby's ribcage, near their waist

- Slide one hand up to the opposite shoulder

- Cup the shoulder

- Slide this hand down the side of the rib cage *(and glide back to where you started)*

- Using your other hand, repeat on the opposite side of the chest

- Repeat 3 times with both hands

Finger rolling

If baby is not so keen, try
again at another time

Tommy Thumb, Tommy Thumb, where are you?
Here I am, here I am, how do you do?

Peter Pointer, Peter Pointer, where are you?
Here I am, here I am, how do you do?

Toby Tall, Toby Tall, where are you?
Here I am, here I am, how do you do?

Ruby Ring, Ruby Ring, where are you?
Here I am, here I am, how do you do?

Baby Small, Baby Small, where are you?
Here I am, here I am, how do you do?

BENEFIT: This can help with teething and snuffles
because of the reflex points in the fingers

- Support one of your baby's hands

- Using your free hand, starting with your baby's thumb

- Roll each finger between your finger and thumb from the base to the tip *(like a caterpillar)*

- At the tip give a gentle hold and move onto the next finger

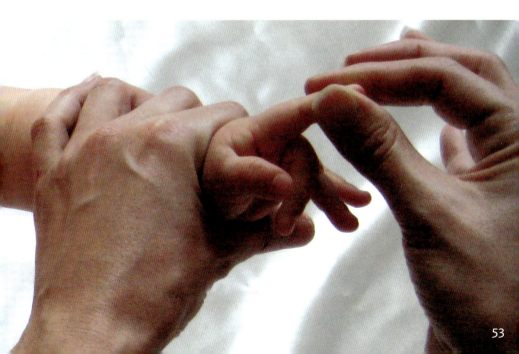

Wrist soother

 Try on the outer wrist if the inner wrist seems too sensitive

BENEFIT: *Improves circulation to the joint*

 Sing this verse to the tune of row, row, your boat:
Wash, wash, wash your hands,
Wash those germs away.
Soap and water does the trick,
To keep them clean all day.

- Cup your baby's hand with your fingers

- Place both of your thumbs on their wrist

- Gently stroke the wrist from the centre to the sides using both of your thumbs

- Repeat 3 times

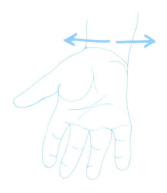

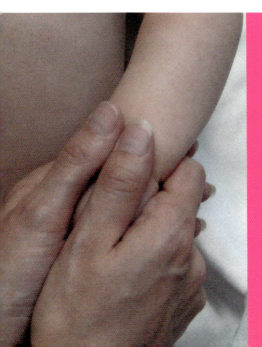

Repeat the Finger Rolling and Wrist Soother on the other arm

Now repeat The Chest and Arm Glide (page 46) to finish the chest massage

Angel kisses

 Avoid the soft spots on your baby's head and don't cover their ears

 Twinkle, twinkle little star,
How I wonder what you are?
Up above the world so high,
Like a diamond in the sky
Twinkle, twinkle little star,
How I wonder what you are?

 BENEFIT: Very relaxing and calming

Using both hands:

- Make small circular movements with the
  pads of your finger tips

- Cover the whole of the head, ending at
  the ears

Ear massage

 If baby is not so keen, try again at another time

Two little eyes to look around,
Two little ears to hear each sound,
One little nose to smell what's sweet,
One little mouth that likes to eat.

BENEFIT: Massage of the auricular points will help to balance all of the body systems

- Using your thumbs and forefingers, gently rub your baby's ears *(starting at the top of the ear)*

- Move down the ears slowly

- Massage the whole of the rim of ears down to the lobes

- To finish, use the pads of the middle fingers and follow the rim of the ears from the top, round and down to the lobe to soothe the nerve endings

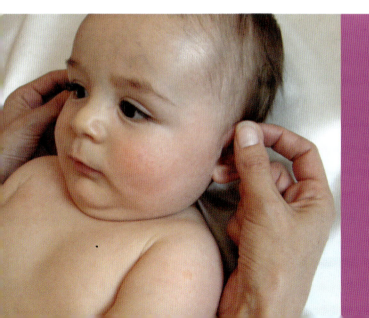

Forehead stroke

Take care not to cover the ears and eyes

BENEFIT: Can help loosen and drain mucus from the sinuses

Some little boys and girls I know
Have freckles on their faces;
Some, freckles on their nose and cheeks
And lots of other places.

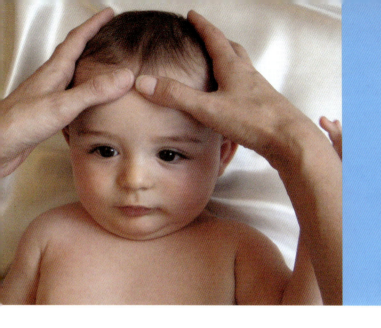

- Place your hands, with fingers spread, on either side of your baby's head

- Place the flat of your thumbs in the middle of their forehead, above the nose

- Gently stroke with your thumbs from the centre of the forehead to the temples

- Repeat 3 times

Nose and cheek stroke

Take care with long nails when stroking the nose and face

There's a big eyed owl,
With a pointed nose,
Two pointed ears and claws for his toes.
He sits in the tree,
And he looks at you;
He flaps his wings,
And says Toowit-Toowoooo!

BENEFIT: Can help loosen and drain mucus from the sinuses

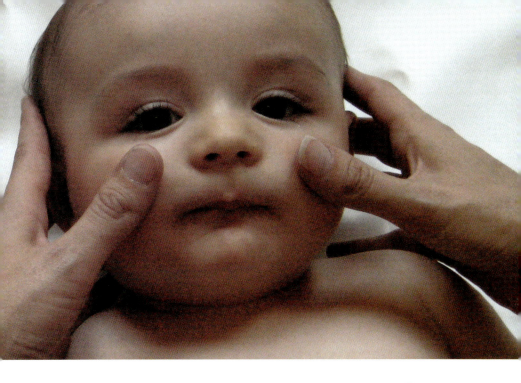

- Place the pads of your thumbs or index fingers at the top of your baby's nose

- Using gentle pressure, stroke down the sides of their nose and along the bottom of the cheek bone, towards their ears

- Repeat 3 times

Back velvet cloak

 Ensure baby's airway is clear

BENEFIT: A soothing stroke to apply the oil and start the back massage

Rain, rain, go away
Come again another day
Little (name) wants to play
Rain, rain, go away,
Come again another day

- Cup your baby's shoulders

- Stroke from the shoulders, down to the ankles *(lighten the stroke from the buttocks to the ankles)*

- Repeat 3 times

Complete back soother

 Never put any pressure on your baby's spine

The little fuzzy caterpillar,
Curled up on a leaf,
Spun her little chrysalis,
And then fell fast asleep.

While she was sleeping,
She dreamed that she could fly,
And later when she woke up
She was a butterfly!

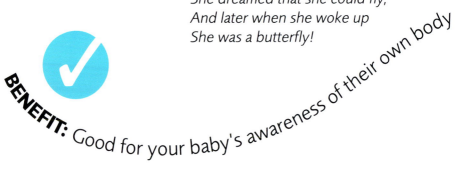

BENEFIT: Good for your baby's awareness of their own body

- Starting at your baby's ankles, stroke up both legs and continue up the back

- Cup their shoulders and glide gently down the arms

- Slide your hands back to the armpits *(try not to tickle here)*

- Slide hands down to the ankles along the sides of their back and legs *(lighten the stroke from the buttocks to the ankles)*

- Repeat 3 times

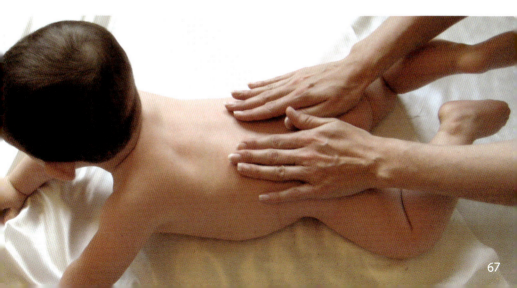

Glide and circle

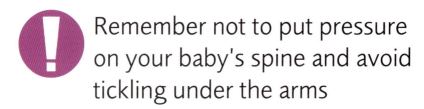

Remember not to put pressure on your baby's spine and avoid tickling under the arms

BENEFIT: *Increases circulation and helps with muscle tone*

Sing a song of sixpence a pocket full of rye,
Four and twenty blackbirds baked in a pie.
When the pie was opened the birds began to sing,
Oh wasn't that a dainty dish to set before the king?

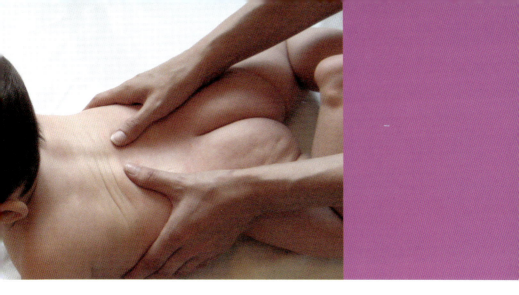

- Starting at your baby's ankles, glide your hands up their legs and over the buttocks

- With the thumbs, or the pads of your first two fingers, make tiny circles either side of the spine, up to the shoulders

- Glide your hands back to the ankles *(lighten the stroke from the buttocks to the ankles)*

- Repeat 3 times *(once baby is used to the back massage)*

Glide and stretch

 Remember not to put pressure on your baby's spine and avoid tickling under the arms

Wee Willie Winkie
Runs through the town
Upstairs and downstairs
In his nightgown
Rapping at the windows
Crying through the lock
"Are the children all in bed?
For it's now eight o'clock."

BENEFIT: Improves posture and general flexibility

- Starting at your baby's ankles, glide your hands up their legs and over the buttocks

- Place your thumbs either side of the spine

- Glide your thumbs from the spine to the side of your baby's body

- Move your hands up slightly after each complete 'stretch' to the side

- Continue up to the shoulders

- Glide your hands back to the ankles *(lighten the stroke from the buttocks to the ankles)*

- Repeat 3 times *(once baby is used to the back massage)*

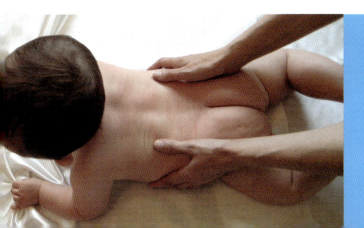

Catspaws

Paws not claws!!

BENEFIT: Deeply soothing for baby and relaxing for you!

Pussy cat, pussy cat
Where have you been?
I've been to London
To visit the Queen.

Pussy cat, pussy cat
What did you there?
I frightened a little mouse
Under a chair!
Meeeeoooowwww

- Use your fingers, opened out like cats paws

- With one hand, stroke down one side of the back, from your baby's shoulders to the buttocks

- Repeat with the other hand on the other side

- Alternating the hands, repeat 3 times with both hands

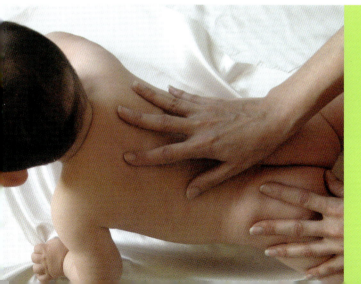

Now repeat The Back Velvet Cloak to finish the back massage

Massage and childhood ailments

Massage can relieve some childhood ailments, reducing the need for lotions and potions.

Colds and snuffles: use the chest and face strokes to help loosen and drain mucus

Colic, wind and constipation: use the Tummy Circle, the Windmill and the Knee Hug around 3 times a day and especially for a colic about an hour before the usual onset

Cradle cap: use the Angel Kisses stroke to apply a small amount of olive oil and leave for a minimum of 15 minutes. Gently comb out the softened flakes and then wash the hair in a mild shampoo

Eczema and psoriasis: massage unbroken skin with a mix of sunflower/olive oil with calendula oil to ease itching and dryness

Sleep problems: introduce massage after a warm bath, as part of the bed-time routine

Teething: use the Finger Rolling and Toe Rolling strokes and the Nose and Cheek Stroke to help alleviate pain

Further reading and resources

'Teach Yourself Baby Massage and Yoga' book, by Anita Epple and Pauline Carpenter

'Rhythm Kids: Fun-time Exercises for Babies' book and CD, by Pauline Carpenter and Anita Epple

'The Music for Dreaming' range of CDs

'Playsongs' range of books and CDs

All available from Touch-Needs Ltd
www.touchneeds.com

Anita Epple

Anita first became interested in baby massage shortly after the birth of her daughter in the late 90s and, from first-hand experience she quickly became aware of its benefits. Since then she has been an enthusiastic and passionate ambassador for baby massage. She teaches parents and professionals in the UK and abroad, she runs an exemplary positive-touch training company and has written several articles and books on the subject, and has even made an appearance on television.

Pauline Carpenter

Pauline first tried massage with her baby and growing children after qualifying as a massage therapist in the early 90s. Realising the many benefits of massage for children, she trained as a Baby Massage Teacher and began teaching other parents this wonderful skill. So impassioned, she went on to support other Baby Massage Teachers and parents through her work with two national associations, the articles and books she has written and her mail order company that supplies the necessary resources needed for baby massage. Pauline also runs a training company that provides excellent positive touch teacher programmes.

Pauline and Anita are Directors of and Trainers for Touch-Learn International Ltd. A training company that provides positive-touch teacher training courses to students all over the world.